HAL•LEONARD
INSTRUMENTAL PLAY-ALONG

AUDIO ACCESS INCLUDED

VIOLIN

QUEEN
UPDATED EDITION

PLAYBACK+
Speed • Pitch • Balance • Loop

To access audio visit:
www.halleonard.com/mylibrary

7758-4514-6041-8216

© Jorgen Angel/CTSIMAGES
Audio arrangements by Peter Deneff

ISBN 978-1-5400-3845-6

HAL•LEONARD®

Visit Hal Leonard Online at
www.halleonard.com

Contact Us:
Hal Leonard
7777 West Bluemound Road
Milwaukee, WI 53213
Email: info@halleonard.com

In Europe contact:
Hal Leonard Europe Limited
42 Wigmore Street
Marylebone, London, W1U 2RN
Email: info@halleonardeurope.com

In Australia contact:
Hal Leonard Australia Pty. Ltd.
4 Lentara Court
Cheltenham, Victoria, 3192 Australia
Email: info@halleonard.com.au

ANOTHER ONE BITES THE DUST

VIOLIN

Words and Music by
JOHN DEACON

CRAZY LITTLE THING CALLED LOVE

VIOLIN

Words and Music by
FREDDIE MERCURY

BICYCLE RACE

VIOLIN

Words and Music by
FREDDIE MERCURY

BOHEMIAN RHAPSODY

VIOLIN

Words and Music by
FREDDIE MERCURY

Hard Rock Shuffle (♩♩ = ♩♪)

Slow Rock

FAT BOTTOMED GIRLS

VIOLIN

Words and Music by
BRIAN MAY

I WANT IT ALL

VIOLIN

Words and Music by FREDDIE MERCURY,
BRIAN MAY, ROGER TAYLOR
and JOHN DEACON

Moderate Rock

DON'T STOP ME NOW

VIOLIN

Words and Music by
FREDDIE MERCURY

D.S. al Coda

CODA

I WANT TO BREAK FREE

VIOLIN

Words and Music by
JOHN DEACON

PLAY THE GAME

VIOLIN

Words and Music by
FREDDIE MERCURY

KILLER QUEEN

VIOLIN

Words and Music by
FREDDIE MERCURY

D.S. al Coda

RADIO GA GA

VIOLIN

Words and Music by
ROGER TAYLOR

SAVE ME

VIOLIN

Words and Music by
BRIAN MAY

SOMEBODY TO LOVE

VIOLIN

Words and Music by
FREDDIE MERCURY

UNDER PRESSURE

Violin

Words and Music by FREDDIE MERCURY,
JOHN DEACON, BRIAN MAY,
ROGER TAYLOR and DAVID BOWIE

WE ARE THE CHAMPIONS

Words and Music by
FREDDIE MERCURY

VIOLIN

WE WILL ROCK YOU

VIOLIN

Words and Music by
BRIAN MAY

YOU'RE MY BEST FRIEND

VIOLIN

Words and Music by
JOHN DEACON